BERNARD W

Who Could ~~~~~ ~~~~~ ~~ ~~~~

Further copies
and more information
available from:

THE FRIENDS OF ST HILARY
ST HILARY CHURCH
PENZANCE

or

MRS C. LOB
JOHN'S CORNER
ROSUDGEON
PENZANCE
TR20 9PJ

Bernard Walke:
A Good Man Who Could Never be Dull

Donald Allchin

p³p

Published in Great Britain 2000
THREE PEAKS PRESS
9 Croesonen Road
Abergavenny,
Monmouthshire NP7 6AE
mail@p3p.org   http://p3p.org

© 2000 by the author
All rights reserved. No part of this publication may be reproduced, stored in a retrieval system, or transmitted in any form by any means except for brief quotation without the prior permission of the publisher.

Designed & set in Joanna at Three Peaks Press

Printed in Wales at Gwasg Dinefwr, Llandybie

A CIP record for this publication
is available from the British Library

ISBN 1–902093–02–X

Foreword

THIS BOOKLET CONTAINS the expanded text of a lecture given at the Church of St Hilary, Cornwall on Monday, July 26th, 1999. It gives an account of the priest who, for twenty-four years, from 1913–1936, was vicar of that parish, and who, in the latter part of that period, made the name of St Hilary known throughout Great Britain.

This renown was due to two very different things. First the plays, and particularly the Christmas plays, which were broadcast year by year from this remote country church in west Cornwall, and secondly the attack made on the church and many of its furnishings by a group of Protestant fanatics in August 1932. Unfortunately it is this latter event which is now, for most of those who remember the name of Bernard Walke at all, the only thing associated with his memory. Here I have tried to give a more full and balanced picture of the man.

Bernard Walke was born in 1874. He was educated at home and at Chichester Theological College. Ordained at the end of the nineteenth century he served a brief first curacy at Walthamstow, in East London. After that his whole ministry was spent in Cornwall, first as a curate at St Ives, then at Polruan. He became vicar of St Hilary in 1913, and he remained there until his resignation in 1936 on account of ill health. His last years were spent at Mevagissey, where he died in June 1941. A few months before his death he was received into the Roman Catholic Church.

I first heard of Bernard Walke as a child, in the years before World War Two when he was still alive and when I came to Cornwall on holiday with my family. I did not of course understand the concern with which his name was mentioned by my parents and grandparents. I have been very grateful in more recent years for the encouragement which has come to me from the vicar and the churchwardens of St Hilary to look more closely into the life and character of this remarkable man. I am also indebted to the Reverend Michael Burgess for sharing with me some of his own deep knowledge of the ministry of Bernard Walke and to Mr Philip Hills of Camborne who is at present actively engaged in detailed research into different aspects of Bernard Walke's life and that of his friend Gerard Collier.

I have quoted in a number of places from Bernard Walke's own autobiographical memoir *Twenty Years at St Hilary*. This book was last republished in 1982 and is now unfortunately out of print. But second hand copies can sometimes be found.

Contents

I   Twenty Years at St Hilary 7
II   The Churchman, the Priest 10
III   The Man of Social Concern 14
IV   The Company of Artists and Writers 18
V   The Company of Saints and Animals 22
VI   Prophetic Power 26

1 Twenty Years at St Hilary

THE MAIN PURPOSE of what is written here is to give, as far as possible, a reasonably rounded and balanced picture of a very remarkable man, a picture which will do justice to the many-sided quality of his character. I know that the picture I give will be tentative and to some extent provisional. It is certainly incomplete, since there is still much to be learnt about Bernard Walke and the circles in which he moved. But I hope here we can make a beginning of seeing him and seeing him in some perspective.

If I wanted a single phrase to sum up Bernard Walke's character, I think I would take some words of Frank Baker, from his book *The Call of Cornwall*; he was "*a good man who could never be dull*". As Frank Baker remarks, such people are rare. It is indeed a remarkable kind of goodness; not heavy and oppressive, but light and lively, liberating and enlivening. W.H.Auden says in one of his essays that he had met many good people who had made him feel bad, but that he had met one or two people who had made him feel quite the reverse, people whom he dared to call holy. He speaks in particular of Charles Williams whom he had met simply in the course of business in a publisher's office. In his presence he said "I felt twice as intelligent, twice as good, and twice as beautiful as I usually am." Only in conversation Auden would say ten times as intelligent, ten times as beautiful etc.! Bernard Walke had precisely this kind of effect on those he met. You felt that he gave you the courage, the freedom to be your own true self.

Unfortunately Bernard Walke is remembered today, if he is remembered at all, for only two things, first the play *Bethlehem*, broadcast every Christmas from 1926 until 1934, second the attack on this church made on August 8th, 1932. For many people, indeed, Bernard Walke is entirely identified with that second unhappy event. But there is very much more to him than that implies. So I shall begin by trying to look at various sides of his character, the churchman, the man of social conscience and social concern, the artist and writer, the friend, the countryman, the lover of animals and plants, and so gradually I shall try to draw together a picture of a man who was at once very varied in his gifts and attitudes, yet deeply one at the core of his being.

I begin with the picture of him which Frank Baker gives in *The Call of Cornwall*. "Of all Father Bernard's friends who were not believers" and there were many of them, "there was not one who ever questioned the depth of his own belief. If I can simplify that belief what did it amount to? The way, the truth and the life, manifested in Jesus Christ, whom he always called 'Our Lord'. When he went in procession on Corpus Christi along the avenue and through the glebe fields of St Hilary, holding high the gilded monstrance, which contained that wafer of bread which is the Body of Christ, not even the most sceptical of critics could question the sweet authority with which he was elevated."

These are two very interesting statements. First, the heart of Bernard Walke's faith is very simple if very profound; it is Jesus Christ himself, the way the truth and the life. As we shall see, it is a very all-embracing faith. But this faith expresses itself in an unwavering belief that the one in whom God and man were perfectly united, the one who lived and died and rose again two thousand years ago in Palestine, is living now in the Church which is his body, and is present with us now in the sacrament which is his body. And Baker speaks of Bernard Walke on Corpus Christi day in rather a remarkable way. He speaks of him as manifesting *a sweet authority*; it is a strange expression.

There is authority here, but it is not oppressive or overpowering. It is attractive, endearing even, and Baker says "this sweet authority with which he was elevated". But, we might reply, it was not the priest who was elevated, it was the Eucharistic Christ, carried high in the monstrance who was elevated, here in the procession through the fields, as at the moment of consecration in the Mass. Baker suggests, that in elevating the host, it is the priest who is elevated. There is a kind of transubstantiation here but it is in us as much as in the sacramental elements. Other food that we eat, we transform into ourselves. This food transforms us into itself; in eating the body of Christ we ourselves become his body.

Baker passes at once from this golden vision of Walke, carrying the blessed sacrament through the beauty of the summer countryside, to the inward daily quality of Walke's existence as a Christian and a priest. He speaks of him as a man "deeply aware of human suffering (and he endured much himself), infinitely tolerant, recognising the sanctified uniqueness of every person he met, a lover of children, animals, a pacifist who gave support to conscientious objectors in prison during the First World War, but who never criticised those who served their country as their country demanded – he had too, enormous faith in humanity, coupled with a sense of humour which enabled him to look at the bewildering human condition and find it good."

Here we have words that tell us something more about the sweet authority of the priest; it is an authority gained through suffering, one's own and that of others. It is an authority which is prepared "to be infinitely tolerant, recognising the sanctified uniqueness of every person we meet". If in the hieratic figure shrouded in the humeral veil, we have an image of Vatican I, here we have another side of Bernard Walke's character, the infinite tolerance of difference, even of profound difference of conviction and belief. Here we have not just Vatican II, but Vatican III. Have we yet caught up with him? Have our churches yet learned that kind of tolerance, which, as we shall see, Bernard Walke was willing to exercise in his longing to serve the poor, the rejected, the excluded members of society?

This was not the tolerance which cares nothing about conviction, nor the optimism which can see good in everything because it has not considered the evil which corrodes our human existence. It is the optimism of grace, the optimism of Julian of Norwich, a writer whom he greatly admired when she was still very little known, who can yet affirm, out of her own vision of the crucified Christ, that "all manner of things shall be well".

11 The Churchman, The Priest

I SHALL START THEN, where surely he would wish us to start, with Bernard Walke the churchman, the priest, the servant of Christ. In this role he is at once paradoxically most dated, most of his own time, but also somehow prophetic. He was of his own time, as part of a whole clerical world which drew its life and inspiration from the Oxford Movement which began in 1833. His grandfather had been a Tractarian pioneer in Cornwall, his father a faithful Tractarian disciple in a parish near the New Forest. Priesthood, the sacraments of the Church, and the life of a country parish, these things were in his blood. On to this he grafted a great respect and love for Rome, and a conviction about the necessary, pivotal role of the Bishop of Rome in the life of the Church. He was what in those days was called "an Anglican Papalist". Canon Miles Brown, in his study of *The Church in Cornwall*, (Truro, 1964), says "he was completely Latin in theology and practice." As we shall find, this is a considerable over-simplification.

What I think was true of Bernard Walke, as of most Catholic-minded clergy of his day, was that he thought of the Church, and above all the Church of Rome, as something constant and unchanging. There was for him no difficulty in knowing what the Roman rite was, what the Roman way of worship was; and it was this that he wanted to introduce into his parish.

How astonished he would be at the changes which have come in the Roman liturgy since Vatican II. Mass is celebrated facing the people, the vernacular is used in worship so as to encourage the active participation of the laity, much greater importance is given to the scriptures and to the sermon. Lay people, both men and women, are encouraged to assist the priest in the distribution of Communion. The change of emphasis in the understanding of Christ's presence in the Mass has made a difference in forms of devotion to Jesus in the blessed sacrament reserved, and so in the reduced prominence given to the service of benediction which meant so much to him. Bernard Walke would be, one imagines, greatly surprised at all these things; and he might well be disconcerted.

On the other hand, how incredulous he would be at some of the changes which have taken place in Anglican worship. So many things which he fought and longed for are now not only permitted but encouraged. Think for instance of the services of Holy Week, which to him and to his friend Sandys Wason, were of such vital importance that they were willing to go to prison for them. Now in many places there is the celebration of Maundy Thursday, with the washing of the feet, and the consecration of Holy oils by the bishop in the cathedral. There are the services of Good Friday, with their veneration of the cross. Above all there is the Easter Vigil with the lighting of the new fire and the paschal candle, and the renewal of baptismal vows.

Such things would have been unthinkable as part of regular Anglican usage in 1910, but how commonly they are practised now. Perhaps even more unbelievable for Walke would have been the existence of an alternative Office Book, *Celebrating Common Prayer*, developed from the Office of the largest of our religious communities, The Society of St Francis. Here is a work, warmly commended by the Archbishop of Canterbury, which contains, amongst other things, the full text of *The Angelus* and also the *Salve Regina* both in Latin and in English. The Church as we know it now, whether in its Roman, Anglican or Free Church manifestations is something very different from the Church which he knew as a young man and as a mature priest. Bernard Walke as a young man, with his friend Sandys Wason and others, had inherited an attitude of intransigent resistance to episcopal authority, which sprang from the struggles over the Public Worship Regulation Act of 1874. This was a struggle which originated in the attempt of the bishops of the time to enforce by law a complete uniformity in Anglican worship, a uniformity which was no longer attainable. It was a struggle which proved long-drawn-out and deeply divisive. In the last years of the nineteenth century there were Anglo-Catholic priests who had gone to prison rather than accept the authority of the courts in these questions.

Bernard Walke inherited these attitudes and continued them, perhaps incongruously, into the nineteen twenties and thirties. The whole complex and lengthy legal conflict over the furnishing and adornment of the church which started in 1932 and which was not finally concluded until 1946, five years after his death, needs to be re-examined. No-one seems to have acted wisely in its beginning. On the one side Bernard Walke seems to have been unnecessarily rigid in his attitude towards the authority of the Consistory court. At times he seems to have been his own worst enemy. By refusing to apply for "faculties", that is official permissions to install the various objects and ornaments which he wished to put in the church, still more by refusing to acknowledge the jurisdiction of the court at all, he left himself undefended, without any possibility of legal redress. Indeed those who attacked the church could claim to be acting in response to the injunctions of the judge, who had ordered that the contested items should be removed.

On the other side the attitude of the court seems to have been extremely short-sighted and pedantic. Beyond all that, one wonders how it was that there seems to have been such a breakdown of confidence between Walke and his bishop, particularly when that bishop was Walter Frere whom he certainly knew personally? There are whole areas of the controversy which I leave on one side but which need further investigation.

What exactly happened on that day in August 1932 is difficult now to make out in detail. We have however Bernard Walke's own vivid and painful description of the events in his *Twenty Years at St Hilarys*. "However much I tried, I could not escape from what was going on around me. I might shut my eyes, but I still saw men standing on the holy altar, hacking at the reredos, or carrying away the image of Our Lady." With his strong sense of history Walke at once felt the parallels between what was going on and what had happened at the time of the Reformation. "I have not yet escaped from the scenes I witnessed that day and possibly never shall; whenever I enter an old country church and see the signs of destruction wrought there in the sixteenth century, I can hear the sounds of hammering and the crash of falling images. The men working this havoc have, in my imagination, the same faces as those who invaded St Hilary that morning in August."

Throughout his life it is clear that Bernard Walke was not a worldly wise man, nor, even in the best sense of the word, an organisation man. He was a man who saw visions and dreamed dreams, but who did not always see how to embody them. But we shall find he was by no means always ineffectual. There was, as we shall discover, another side to his understanding of priesthood which he seems to have held from the very beginning of his ministry, which was of vital importance to him. This was his practical conviction that to be an effective pastor he needed to have a direct, personal experience of the working life of his parishioners. So, during his brief second curacy at St Ives, and during his longer time at Polruan, he would go out with the fishermen in their boats, would sign on, on the tramp steamers sailing from Fowey on their coastal journeys, in order to experience for himself the life of his people.

This was an ideal of identification with the poor, which Bernard Walke, with others, shared with the earliest members of the Society of the Divine Compassion, the first Franciscan brotherhood to be established in the Church of England at the end of the nineteenth century. The S.D.C. was coming into existence in east London in the very years when Bernard Walke was exercising his first ministry in Walthamstow. The brotherhood was one whose Christian Socialist aspirations were very close to those of Bernard Walke himself. As we shall see, such ideals were to influence him throughout the course of his ministry and we are not surprised to find, that one of his closest collaborators at St Hilary, Grace Costin, who was, for a time, in charge of the children's home there, was herself, later in life, to found a small Franciscan community. This community lived in Devon, and its life of simplicity and informality, "of happiness and equality", was imbued with deeply held pacifist convictions which again remind us of St Hilary and its vicar.

III The Man of Social Concern

THUS WE COME to our second main consideration of Bernard Walke's character, seeing him as a man of social conscience and social concern. A man who is always trying to find how it is that the Christian faith may be embodied not only in our worship but in the daily life of our world.

In *Twenty Years at St Hilary*, in Walke's own account of these things, there seem to be three main phases to this part of his story. The first begins in the last years of World War One and is related to his feeling that he needed to be more articulate and more explicit in speaking about the reasons for his peace testimony, his pacifism. Partly through the influence of members of the Society of Friends, he joined the ecumenical Fellowship of Reconciliation, at that time a predominantly free church and Quaker society. His book contains some vivid, lively accounts of rowdy meetings held in Penzance in the last months of 1917 and early in 1918, when pacifist ideas could be relied on to produce passionate and violent reactions in a general audience.

This work for peace went on after the war. It brought him into attempts to organise relief and aid for Russia, suffering the threat of famine as a result of the civil war which followed the October Revolution; it also brought him into prayers for peace and reconciliation in Ireland, a country also on the brink of civil war. It is the Quaker, Arthur Jenkins, who takes the initiative here, saying "We are a Celtic people and we owe the Christian faith to the Irish saints and missionaries who crossed over to Cornwall. Is Cornwall going to make no effort... to repay the debt in this time of violent distress?"

We have a picture of unprecedented ecumenical gatherings for prayer at this time "and among others who welcomed these efforts for reconciliation between the two countries was the Roman Catholic priest in Truro (who was himself an Irishman), who invited us to his church, where Quakers, non-conformists, members of the Church of England, and Catholics, could meet for an hour of silence before the Blessed Sacrament, until these meetings in a Catholic church were ordered to cease." Among those with whom Walke worked was a noted Welsh pacifist G.M. Lloyd Davies, a man of liberal theological views who was for a time a Presbyterian minister and who was instrumental in making contact between Lloyd George and the leaders of Sinn Fein. Bernard Walke describes him "as another Celt, he shared our sense of responsibility." It is interesting that we find Walke aware of his Celticness here in a social and political context rather than an ecclesiastical one.

The second phase in this period of Walke's life is linked with his longing to set up some kind of interdenominational lay order which could work for a more just society. Here, for him, the relation of the Eucharist to society as a whole was of fundamental importance. "At the moment of his farewell, when the Son of God was to leave his friends he had gathered round him, he had set up a common table, where men might meet, and sharing in his gifts of bread and wine, find him present with them. For those who share in the gift of the *Corpus Domini* – the body of God – there must be a way, I thought, in which they could share more completely in the daily things of life." Bernard Walke it seems had been influenced by the theology of F.D. Maurice, as well as by the theology of E.B. Pusey.

Twenty Years at St Hilary gives an account of a conference held at St Hilary to which people of very different viewpoints came. Among them was the young presbyterian minister, William Paton, who was to become one of the outstanding ecumenical statesmen of the twentieth century. Out of this meeting there came a scheme for an association, *Brethren of the Common Table*. This plan seems to have been an impressive one and for a time it aroused much interest and branches of the association were formed as far away as London. But in the end, apparently, these hopes proved to be insubstantial.

The third phase in this period of Walke's life is linked directly with two things. First there was the time of economic and social distress in Cornwall which followed the end of the war, a time of mass unemployment, the collapse of the mining industry and widespread poverty and malnutrition. Second, there was the arrival in his life of a friend who was to influence him greatly, Gerard Collier.

Gerard Collier was born in 1878, and was thus four years younger than Walke. He came from a family which had long been active in public life. His father had been a Liberal MP, involved in the early years of the London County Council. His grandfather and great grandfather had both been members of parliament for Plymouth. Gerard Collier inherited from his family this sense of a calling to the service of society at large. Already in his youth people saw some special gift in him. A.C. Benson, his house-master at Eton, speaks of him with special affection. After a brilliant career at Balliol College Oxford, where he gained a first in history, he became more and more involved in work for peace. This took him into the time of the First World War and to the foundation of the Fellowship of Reconciliation. In 1919 after a time of illness he came with his wife and children and settled at Marazion, not far from St Hilary. He and Bernard Walke quickly became very close friends; Walke's admiration for him was unbounded.

Among other things the two men began to consider how it was that they should act in Cornwall, how they could seek to put their ideals into practice there. Would it be possible they wondered to initiate some kind of workers' co-operative amongst the miners? Once again the Society of Friends plays a central role. Many of the early gatherings which Collier and Walke were involved in, to do with this project, took place in the Friends Meeting House in Redruth, "a building with which I was familiar, having often attended there in the stormy days during the war". There were planning meetings and also prayer meetings, where the attitude of the miners themselves greatly impressed Bernard Walke. "Their amens and alleluias are sharp and incisive – as the ring of the pick against the naked rock... their prayers are often eloquent of the longing of the human heart for God, the cries of men who have spent their lives in darkness and whose souls long for light and splendour.... Here was a people, who unlike many industrial workers, have never lost faith in God. The fire that John Wesley kindled was not altogether extinguished."

This time Walke, Collier and their Quaker friend Arthur Jenkins, were joined by others including Thomas Attlee, brother of the future Prime Minister and initiator of the work of the WEA in Cornwall. The scheme which was devised was to bring the workers together into a co-operative enterprise to reopen one of the many closed mines near Scorrier. It got at least an initial commendation from the leaders of all the churches in Cornwall (with the exception of the Roman Catholics) with the Bishop Guy Warman at their head, and it took Bernard Walke to London to preach at the King's Weigh House Church a sermon on "Religion and Industry in Cornwall". Once again, however, such plans were doomed to come to nothing, and Walke at least suggests that dismay over this failure was one of the factors which hastened on Gerard Collier's death from tuberculosis in April 1923 at the age of forty-four.

Something of the anguish felt at that death of a greatly gifted man may be sensed in the strange powerful, disturbing figure of the dead Christ which Ernest Procter painted as a memorial to him and which is now placed at the west end of the church, over the Altar of All Souls. It is a picture which also surely reflects Procter's own experience as a Quaker in the Friends Ambulance Brigade during the latter years of the war. In his account of the life of Gerard Collier, Philip Hills remarks of it, "It stands in testament to the close friendship of two outstanding men of faith, Gerard Collier and Bernard Walke. With the artist Ernest Procter it is a memorial to the fellowship of peace in Christ. All three men were Christian pacifists."

IV The Company of Artists and Writers

IF BERNARD WALKE FOUND it difficult to know how to proceed in matters involving committees and administration, it is clear that he and his wife felt themselves altogether at home in the company of artists and writers. Here we come to another very important element of their life at St Hilary, their friendship and collaboration with members of the Newlyn School of painting which flourished from the 1890s until at least the time of the Second World War. From the moment of their arrival onwards, Bernard and Annie Walke found intimate friends and supporters there.

This identification with what would then have been considered a very unconventional group of people, rather than with the local squirearchy, or indeed with the neighbouring clergy, was deepened during the years of the war when the Walkes found themselves particularly isolated on account of their pacifist stance. Here their views were shared by many members of the Newlyn school. Harold Knight for instance, was a conscientious objector and Ernest Procter as we have seen served in the Friends Ambulance Brigade. Many of these friendships lasted for a lifetime and brought the Walkes into close contact with painters of the stature of Dame Laura Knight and Sir Alfred Munnings, the future president of the Royal Academy. With the current growth in interest in the work of the Newlyn School and with the new studies of their work which are appearing, we are sure to hear more of the part which the Walkes played in their life as a group, not least of course in the case of those who shared actively in the decoration of this church. That is a theme to which we shall come back.

If Bernard Walke and his wife found themselves at home with painters, the same would of course be true of the world of writers. Bernard Walke himself was, after all, an artist in words and not in line and colour. Here again there were friends who welcomed them to St Hilary on their very first arrival, notably Compton

Mackenzie and his wife Faith. Later they were to receive visits from Walter de la Mare and George Bernard Shaw, amongst others. The latter seems to have come in connection with the broadcast plays which from 1926 onwards were to become a major feature in Bernard Walke's life and which reveal something of his considerable capacities as a writer.

Certainly until the incidents of August 1932, these broadcast plays, in particular the Christmas play *Bethlehem*, were the principal cause of Bernard Walke's name being known to the general public. As in other areas of Bernard's life here is a field which needs to be examined in detail. At least we may say this; as a piece of outside broadcasting the Christmas plays from St Hilary had no precedent. It is difficult for us now to realise how much it meant for people to hear voices coming from a place so far from London, and to hear as a local listener put it "the voices of ordinary village folk presented for the whole of the nation to listen to." Such "non-standard English" was very little heard on the BBC at that time. Again Bernard Walke was flying in the face of established convention in agreeing to the plays being broadcast at all. For almost ten years the plays became an essential part of Christmas broadcasting, an early equivalent of the *Nine Lessons and Carols* of recent years.

One rather unexpected account of the impression that the Christmas plays made in these years comes from the Welsh pacifist minister, George M. Lloyd Davies who had worked with Bernard Walke in 1921 in the attempt to make contacts between Britain and Ireland. Davies had spent some time in the summer of 1930, staying on Bardsey Island, the island of the twenty thousand saints, as it is called, off the westernmost tip of North Wales, and had been greatly struck by his time there. The island then was still a functioning community of farming and fishing people. For whatever reason Davies decided to go back again just before Christmas, despite the possibility that at that time of the year the weather could cut him off from the mainland for weeks. There, to his intense surprise, in an entirely Welsh-speaking environment, he found that someone had been given a second hand wireless set.

So he heard Bernard Walke's voice, the voice of a friend and the voices of his parishioners. "It seemed so right, both in its setting and receiving, the accent of Cornish farm folk, the voices of children, the unsophisticated drama and diction of the players... Here were crofters and lighthousemen, receiving and pondering that perennial story... here it seemed easy to believe that the gulf that divided nations and parties and sects and societies could be crossed as naturally as the islanders crossed to the mainland."

Listening to the recording of the ninth and last performance, made in 1934, I was impressed above all by the play as a total work of art, and quite consciously and explicitly as a work of sacred art, conceived primarily as an act of corporate worship, not an act either of instruction or entertainment performed by a few on behalf of many. There is no attempt here at a realistic recreation of first century Palestine; rather we have a sacramental action intended to involve all those present in the eternal meaning and significance of what happened then and what is happening now. Speaking today to people who as children had taken part in that play, or who remembered brothers or sisters or parents or friends taking part, I was struck by the way in which at this distance of time the play was still real to them and still felt to be something which belongs to them. Of course the plays actually involved not only the performers, though they were numerous, actors, singers, dancers, bell-ringers, but also all the others who decorated the church for the occasion and who made the costumes and who prepared the feast which took place afterwards. The play in this way became a community event and that is how it is remembered, sixty years later.

The existence of the plays (for it is important to remember that there were a number of other plays which were also performed, some of which were also broadcast, notable among them *The Eve of All Souls*) suggest that Bernard Walke had at least in this respect, managed to bridge the gulf between himself and the people of his parish and to convey his vision and his faith to some of them, more than he himself always realised, and certainly more than outsiders usually understood.

Filson Young, the producer who was responsible for the broadcasting of the plays, writing of them in 1936 at the time of Walke's resignation from the parish, asks what was the cause of the widespread interest they aroused and the profound influence they had on so many listeners. He begins with Walke's own "character and genius...the deep reality of the religious faith that is the inspiration of his life and ministry," and he then goes on to speak of "the close bond between the author and the players. Not only as their parish priest but as their friend he had been so intimately a part of their very lives...". Here especially Bernard Walke's gift of bringing together people of different ages and totally different social backgrounds was revealed. The three plays which were published by Fabers in 1939, *The Upper Chamber*, *The Eve of All Souls* and *The Stranger at St Hilary*, a reworking of the Christmas theme, are all a remarkable witness to this gift.

All this makes the actions of the Church authorities in countenancing and even in some ways furthering the disruptive acts of the protestors in August 1932 still more puzzling. In face of the plays, these imaginative acts of faith and worship, which when broadcast communicated something of the meaning of the Christian faith to a very large audience, it is difficult to think that the illegalities condemned by the Consistory Court, the stone altars, the statues, the tabernacles which had been introduced into the building without proper legal permission could be considered all that important. It shows, to say the least, a very strange sense of proportion.

V The Company of Saints and Animals

WE HAVE BEEN LOOKING at various sides of Bernard Walke's life and activity as vicar of St Hilary. Behind all this there was the man himself, and I want finally to look at one aspect of his inner character which seems to me of particular importance, and which helps us to gain some idea of how it was he managed to hold together the different facets of his personality.

Bernard Walke was a countryman, with a deep love and understanding of country people, and also of the whole living world of nature, the world of trees and plants, of animals and birds. His father had been vicar of a country parish, and Bernard grew up at home, with his two brothers, in his case not going to school at all, but nominally being taught the classics by his father.

"I do not regret these days of idleness... the son of a parsonage whose youth is spent in the country among its people, has many advantages. He knows no social distinctions; he is as much at home in the farm or in the cottage of the labourer as in the house of the squire, and he inherits a tradition of culture as naturally as he finds himself a person of importance in the life of the village."

Personally he recognises that he lost something in his failure to receive scholarship and learning, but "on the other hand such a life ensures a freedom from a tradition which often leaves an indelible mark upon the outlook and personality of those who share it. In my own case the result of such an upbringing has been that throughout my life I have repeatedly questioned many of the accepted formulas of society. If I had been endowed with a public school education with its code of morals or rather of good and bad form, I would, without doubt have been saved many of those indecisions which have haunted my life." Walke remained throughout his life a very independent man, as we have already seen in his close collaboration with Quakers and Non-conformists. It is striking that the only reference to a contemporary theologian in his book is a reference to the radical Catholic modernist, George Tyrrell.

Growing up in a pre-industrial world, Walke seems to have inherited a great delight in and love for ordinary people. It was this which made him, in the first place, such a remarkable priest, and which meant that despite all the misunderstandings about Roman practices, he remained in such good relations with the great majority of his congregation. But more than, or perhaps behind and beneath, that there was his sense of closeness to the whole living world, the world of animals, the world of nature. This is one of the sides of his character which comes out strongly in his autobiography. There is a whole chapter devoted to donkeys, a chapter which concludes with a kind of telepathic incident which clearly moved and shook him. He describes how a donkey which had lived with them and worked with them had to be sent away to a farm some ten miles off, and how one year after he had been looking at pictures of the donkey and thinking of him, in the middle of the night the donkey arrived. "Whether the tender thoughts that I had had towards him that evening had led him across the causeway at Hayle, along the lanes through St Erth village, to bray beneath my window, or whether his setting out and coming was made known to me I cannot tell. It is again too difficult a problem for me to solve. If these things are true, the world we live in is not the safe place we sometimes imagine it to be."

One of the most beautiful passages in *Twenty Years at St Hilary* comes towards its end where Walke speaks of his delight in the flowers and plants and birds of autumn. "Birds are more friendly at this season than in the spring, when they are busy with their own affairs... a nestful of young robins who were hatched in the garden come and stare as if they would say, since we are spending the winter with you it's as well to be friendly". "Each day they become more impudent, lighting on my foot and taking ants from the stone seat where I am sitting... I am aware of the increased friendliness among all living things. The children congregate in flocks... Men returning from work lean over gateways, and talk with passersby of the harvest of the year which is coming to a close..."

I am aware of the increased friendliness among all living things. Perhaps this is one of the most important words of Bernard Walke to our anxious, perilous, threatened, frenetic world. It is a word which is spoken again by the most remarkable and to my mind the most significant series of paintings which the Church of St Hilary contains, the paintings of the Cornish saints around the pulpit and the choir stalls, as Bernard Walke calls it "the collective work of Ernest Procter, Dod Procter, Annie Walke, Harold Harvey, Norman Garstin, Harold Knight and Gladys Hynes".

As with so many elements in this story there is investigation here which still needs to be done, into the paintings themselves, taken individually and as a group, and into the subjects which they depict. One thing is clear, as Bernard Walke points out, many of the scenes depicted "tell of the love of saints for the creatures..." St Endelienta drawn to her resting place by six young calves; St Piran with his first disciples, a badger, a bear and a fox; St Petroc saving the faun from the hounds. Around the pulpit there are three of the most striking pieces, all the work of Ernest Procter, St Neot impounding the crows at the time of Mass, St Kevin with not one but two bird's nests in his outstretched hands and St Mawes with his sheep and the precious red book. Then in the chancel there is perhaps the most interesting of them all. In Bernard Walke's words "it shows how St Fingar, after having killed a stag, knelt at a forest pool to wash his hands and seeing himself reflected in the still water, dedicated his beauty to the service of God."

What no-one can miss who reads the memoir carefully, is the curious parallel between this story and what Bernard Walke tells of an incident in his own youth. He tells us that he had been following a stag hunt. The stag had not been killed but had taken refuge in deep water where the huntsmen and dogs could not get at it. "After the field had ridden away it was very quiet and as I lay in the heather watching the stag with the hind close up to his flanks, I could hear the sucking sound as he bent his head to drink.

After a time I ceased to be interested in the stag and was conscious only, as people often are when they are very young, of being intensely sad. The horse at my side started and in looking around I saw the stag, with the hind following, come out of the water and trot slowly to a hill not far from where I lay. There they stood, and as I looked at them I became alive to the beauty of everything round me and the thought of the stupidity of man who would destroy its fairness in his lust to hunt and to kill."

Then "the stag threw back his head and brayed defiance." At that moment Bernard Walke knew that he had finished with hunting forever. "I made no vows but vows were then made for me, that I should be, else sinning greatly, a dedicated spirit." (William Wordsworth).

In the one story there is a young man who has killed a stag in the forest and who comes to wash his hands. In the other there is a young man who has followed the hunt to its inconclusive finish, and then stays to see what happens. But in both we have a moment of sudden conversion, a moment of the overwhelming perception of the beauty of God shining out in all around, and in themselves, which makes them exclaim "Such beauty is of too great value to be wasted on hunting and feasting." Both young men find themselves, whether they know it or not, dedicated forever to the service of that beauty.

In focusing attention on this group of paintings of Celtic saints, I do not wish to suggest that Bernard Walke was an altogether ardent advocate of what we now call Celtic Christianity. For though in the account of the church which he wrote in 1929, he speaks of the stories of the saints as revealing "something of the simplicity and beauty of the lives of these men and women to whom Cornwall owes so much", in *Twenty Years at St Hilary*, he speaks in more guarded terms, "these and other strange old stories are whimsical memories of men and women, who in those dim pagan days landed on our shores." Perhaps in the Anglicanism of his day, to be too pro-Celtic meant to be strongly anti-Roman, and that he would never consent to be. And after all, in the church at St Hilary, St Francis and St Joan of Arc have as large a place as the Celtic saints.

But in the choice of subjects for this series of paintings Bernard Walke has revealed something of his own deepest nature, his sense of kinship and affinity with the whole living world of which he is part, his sense of its beauty and of its sacred, yet infinitely fragile quality, its capacity to reveal the glory and indeed the beauty of the Creator of all to us. In these as in other ways he has shown himself to be deeply at one, consciously or unconsciously, with the saints of those early centuries who moved easily between Brittany and Cornwall and Wales and Ireland. In him something of their strangeness and attractiveness seems to be present and at work. In him we sense their sweet authority, an authority which far from oppressing enlivens and makes free. It is this quality which has made those early Celtic centuries so powerfully attractive in recent years, to men and women in places as far away as New Zealand and Australia, Texas and New York.

It is this enlivening quality which Frank Baker remembers above all else in Bernard Walke. In one place he writes, "it is safe to say that Ber Walke infected everyone who met him with his own unconditional love of life and people. And more: they caught from him an awareness of a state of being, which reduced materialism to dry ashes." In another he says "what he did to me, as to many others, was something one never forgets. He made me feel that I had an important part to play in life, and this part was mine and mine alone. All I had to do was to interpret the script that the Creator had handed to me. In Ber's world everyone played an essential role... that was the feeling one had in Ber's study on Sunday morning, after the Mass in the beautiful flower-filled church, with all its contemporary paintings, with its great wooden crucifix, and Ernest Procter's pathetic altar of the dead..." That is the church which we still have with us, and which still speaks to us, in this twenty-first century with the voice of this strange, compelling and endearing man.

VI Prophetic Power

IN *A History of English Christianity, 1920-1985*, Adrian Hastings speaks in high praise of two very unconventional Anglican missionary priests of the first half of the twentieth century, Arthur Shearly Cripps in Rhodesia, and C.F. Andrews, the friend of Gandhi, in India, seeing them both as men of prophetic power. Compared with Shearly Cripps and C.F. Andrews, Bernard Walke's life for all its incidents, must seem quiet, assured, almost conventional. Yet there are things which Hastings says about his two heroes, which we might well apply to Walke, things which enable us to situate in its true context that strange moment of battle between light and darkness which took place in the Church of St Hilary on August 8th 1932. "They moved out from the centre of an Establishment, powerful, Erastian, conformist, to challenge it most absolutely... by the sheer quality of a religious commitment, love of neighbour, intellectual integrity, a flow of poetry affecting every aspect of life." Surely in these last phrases we may see an almost uncannily accurate portrait of the vicar of this parish: "the sheer quality of a religious commitment, love of neighbour, intellectual integrity, a flow of poetry affecting every aspect of life."

In the case of the two missionaries it was their capacity to enter into, to feel with the altogether despised and ignored, whether an Indian untouchable or an African labourer, which, in Hastings' judgement, most showed their identification with Christ. Do we not see in the gesture of Bernard Walke taking off his shirt in order to clothe the old dying tin miner, ashamed to die and go before his Maker in quite such poverty and disarray, a comparable moment of identification with the poorest, the most totally other? Here was a man whose living goodness caught the attention of all, whose integrity of life was such that the powers of darkness felt bound to attack it, a man who demands of us, as we enter a new century, a new millennium, our attention, our love, our admiration, our concern, for in him too we see, "a prophetic power", a power which can lead us into that new time which is coming.

MADE AND PRINTED IN WALES BY
GWASG DINEFWR PRESS
LLANDYBIE FOR
THREE PEAKS PRESS
9 CROESONEN ROAD, ABERGAVENNY,
MONMOUTHSHIRE NP7 6AE